UNEARTH
HISTORY

Philip Steele
Consultant: Richard Platt

Miles
Kelly

CONTENTS

◀ Hundreds of terra-cotta soldiers, horses, and chariots were discovered in Shandong, China, in 2002. The soldiers were once painted in bright colors.

ACCIDENTAL Finds

The discovery of an ancient site helps archeologists to uncover the past. Sometimes ordinary people come face to face with history unexpectedly. A farmer may uncover Egyptian pottery, a caver may stumble across Native American arrowheads, or a metal detector may find a hoard of Roman silver. Each piece gives an insight into the history of human life.

THE FACE OF POWER

The Crosby Garrett helmet was found in 2010 in Cumbria, England, using a metal detector. It dates back to between the 1st and 3rd centuries AD. This brass cavalry helmet would never have been practical for the battlefield. It was probably made for the parade ground, or for public ceremonies. The face acted as a visor and the wearer would have struck awe into all who saw him, his face shining like a god.

A SHIP IN MANHATTAN

In 2010, workers building the new World Trade Center in New York City, U.S., uncovered the remains of a wooden ship, with a hull that was 32.2 ft (9.8 m) long. Tests on the wood showed that it dates back to the 1770s, the time of the American Revolution. The sailing ship was a locally built sloop. It had probably traded up and down the Hudson River or along the coast.

SAXON GOLD

In 2009, a metal detector made an incredible discovery—the Staffordshire Hoard. It included more than 3,500 items of gold, silver, and garnets. The artifacts date back to the 7th or 8th century—the time of the kingdom of Mercia. This hoard is the largest collection of Anglo-Saxon gold and silver ever found.

Sacred scrolls

From 1946 to 1947, two shepherds living near the shores of the Dead Sea, Palestine, discovered precious scrolls in some ancient caves. By 1956, 972 separate texts had been identified. They were written between 150 BC and AD 70 and include parts of the Hebrew Bible and other writings about religious sects.

A Roman piggy bank

In 2010, a pottery jar was uncovered by metal detecting in Frome, England. It contained 52,503 Roman coins, dating from AD 253–305. Many of the coins were from the time of Carausius, an army commander of Celtic origin who proclaimed himself breakaway Roman emperor in AD 286.

PLANNING A DIG

Archeological digs are carried out by museums, universities, and historical societies. Digs can often last for months. Archeologists and volunteers use special tools so as not to damage any of the finds during excavation.

LEGENDARY Prizes

▶ Schliemann found this stunning gold mask at Mycenae in Greece.

The greatest archeological finds can change the way we think about the past. Some explorers have devoted many years of their lives to searching for the ultimate sites. Significant discoveries may be in challenging locations, massive in size, incredibly ancient, or even solve a historical puzzle.

Monster move

The big dig—this is the site of Kalhu or Nimrud, in modern Iraq. Here stood the splendid palace of King Ashurnasirpal II, who ruled the Assyrian Empire from 883 to 859 BC. Inside were giant statues of lions and winged bulls with human heads, to guard the king against evil. In 1847 archeologist Austen Henry Layard (1817–1894) decided to move two of these to the British Museum in London, U.K.

Each giant statue weighed about 10 tons. It took 300 men to haul them to the bank of the River Tigris—an epic task!

ALONG WITH THE TERRA-COTTA ARMY, 11 TERRA-COTTA ACROBATS AND STRONGMEN WERE UNCOVERED.

▲ A bearded human head, wearing a sacred headdress, tops the 13-ft- (4-m-) high winged bull statue.

The incredible hunch

Heinrich Schliemann (1822–1890) had always been fascinated by the legends of Greece and Troy. As an archeologist he was an amateur. His methods were wrong and his dating was incorrect—but he was a very lucky man. He located and excavated the ancient site of Troy at Hisarlik, in Turkey. This made people realize that the *Iliad*, an epic poem about the Trojan War, might be based upon events that really took place, thousands of years ago.

Alongside Tutankhamun's coffin, Carter discovered 2,000 treasures.

▶ This dazzling gold mask covered the face of Tutankhamun's mummy.

A glint of gold

The most famous discovery in archeological history began on November 4, 1922, when the archeologist Howard Carter (1874–1939) located a tomb in the Valley of the Kings, in southern Egypt. The valley had been a secret burial ground for Egypt's rulers. The tomb belonged to a young pharaoh called Tutankhamun (c. 1341–1323 BC).

◀◀ The pits containing the life-sized model soldiers were discovered in 1974.

Army of ghosts

In 246 BC, 700,000 workers in Xi'an, China, were given an awesome task— to build a tomb for the first Chinese emperor, Qin Shi Huangdi, and then produce a great army to guard it and protect him in the afterlife. The workers set about creating statues of troops from terra-cotta (baked clay).

◀ In all, there may have been 8,000 model soldiers, 670 horses, and 130 chariots in the burial pits.

MIGHTY
Monuments

Throughout history, people have raised massive buildings, monuments, and statues. The builder's aim has been to create a sense of respect, terror, wonder, or delight. For archeologists, they help to show how past societies lived.

Chartres Cathedral

The glorious Rose Window at Chartres Cathedral in France was built around 1215.

TEMPLE OF THE SERPENT

Chichén Itzá in Mexico was a great city of the Maya and Toltec peoples, occupied between the 8th and 13th centuries AD. In its later years, a great stepped pyramid was built there as a temple to the Feathered Serpent god. A snake, carved in stone, adorns the stairways, and twice each year the Sun casts strange snakelike shadows on the northern steps. The monument later became known in Spanish as *el Castillo*, meaning "the Castle."

ISLAND GUARDIANS

The first European seafarers to reach the coasts of the remote Pacific island of Rapa Nui ("Easter Island") were mystified by huge stone statues, called Moai. They were carved by the Polynesians who lived there between 1200 and 1680. The tallest statue is 33 ft (10 m) high and the heaviest weighs 86 tons.

Chichén Itzá

The pyramid and its platform have one step for each day of the year.

EASTER ISLAND MOAI

887 Moai have survived on Easter Island. They represent ancestors who became gods.

Power and praise

Europe's medieval Christian cathedrals were built with massive towers to impress people with the power of God, or with tall spires pointing to the heavens. Inside were golden altars and stained-glass windows to dazzle the eye or to tell picture stories of the saints. These buildings, such as Chartres Cathedral, attracted thousands of pilgrims from across Europe.

MACHINE-AGE MAGIC

Back in 1930, this soaring skyscraper was the world's tallest building. It is still one of the most spectacular sights in New York City, U.S., and a historical landmark. It was originally the headquarters of the giant car manufacturing corporation, Chrysler.

Chrysler Building

This magnificent building has 77 floors and is 1,046 ft (319 m) high.

EVERLASTING LOVE

Its white marble walls are inlaid with gems, its tall towers, or minarets, are graceful and slender, and its domes are reflected in still pools of water. This is the Taj Mahal at Agra, India, and it is believed by many to be the most beautiful building in the world. Constructed between 1630 and 1653, it was built as a tomb to commemorate the love Mughal emperor of India, Shah Jahan, felt for his deceased wife, Mumtaz Mahal. In 1666, Shah Jahan also died and was buried next to his wife.

Taj Mahal

Over 1,000 elephants were used to haul marble to the site.

SECRETS OF STONE

The great pillars of Stonehenge rise from Salisbury Plain in southern England. The stones line up with the positions of the Sun and stars during the year. Stonehenge was probably a site for sacred rituals and was built in several stages between about 2600 and 1600 BC.

STONEHENGE

Some believe that Stonehenge was a calendar, a temple of the Sun, or a center of healing.

ANCIENT Empires

The great empires of the past once wielded immense power, governing vast areas and amassing great wealth. However, with their crumbling monuments all around, we are reminded that no power lasts forever—every empire must fall.

Defending the empire

Power attracts enemies, so empires need strong defenses. The Chinese emperors feared invasion by tribes who lived to the north. Between the 3rd century BC and the 16th century AD they built the world's longest network of fortifications—the Great Wall of China. The wall also served as an east-west route for trade and communications. Although impressive, the Great Wall failed to stop the Mongol invasion of China in the 1200s.

▲ Thousands of miles long, the original wall still stands in places, but some sections have been rebuilt in modern times.

IVORY QUEEN

Great empires often produced awesome works of art. This graceful head represents Queen Idia, the mother of Esigie who ruled the Benin Empire (in modern Nigeria) from 1504 to 1550. Many empires thrived in Africa before their lands were seized by European empire-builders in the 1800s and 1900s.

◀ This ivory mask of Queen Idia is now at the Metropolitan Museum of Art, New York, U.S.

The King of Kings

The ruins of Persepolis still stand in southwest Iran. This was the city of Darius the Great, ruler of the Persian Empire from 522 to 486 BC. Persian lands eventually stretched from Western and Central Asia to Europe and North Africa. It was the biggest empire the world had ever known, ruling about 50 million people.

▼ This bas-relief (projecting image) in Persepolis, Iran, shows people climbing the stairs with offerings for Darius the Great.

DURING THE MING DYNASTY (1368–1644), ONE MILLION SOLDIERS WERE STATIONED ALONG THE GREAT WALL OF CHINA.

Emperor of the Sun

An excited crowd gathers in an ancient Inca fortress at Cuzco, Peru, to watch a spectacular reenactment of the Sun festival of Inti Raymi. In the 1400s and early 1500s, the Inca Empire, called Tawantinsuyu, covered 2,403 mi (3,867 km) of South American coastal strip and mountains. The emperor, or Sapa Inca, was held in awe. He was believed to be a god, descended from the Sun. Each year he made sacrifices at the festival, which was held on June 24 (midwinter in the Southern Hemisphere).

▶ A modern presentation of the ancient Inca festival still impresses the crowds.

Power over peoples

Empires are many lands brought together under a single ruler or government. They depend not only on military power but also on administration, laws, and communications. These skills first came together in the Middle East. The world's very first empire was ruled by the city of Akkad, Mesopotamia, and was founded in 2334 BC by a ruler called Sharrum-Kin or Sargon I. It stretched from the Mediterranean Sea to the Persian Gulf, but had collapsed by about 2160 BC.

◀ This copper head may represent Sargon I, but it is more likely to be his grandson Naram-Sin, who died in 2218 BC.

Code BREAKERS

If we are to travel back in history, we need to know the languages of the distant past. Often the words and scripts are long forgotten. They appear as strange symbols carved on rocks, tombs, or temples. Only language experts can solve these mysteries. Their work may take a lifetime, but if they succeed in cracking the code, they open up a window into the past.

Pris: Helår 15: 50.

ALLERS
FAMILJ-JOU

Allers Familj-Journals tryckeri-aktiebolag, Hälsingbo

N:r 29.

Just som de... ...e vetenskapsmannens var i färd med
...hår när, att hon

The Rosetta riddle

In 1799 a slab of black stone was found at Rosetta (Rashid) in Egypt. It had been carved in three different scripts in 196 BC to mark the start of a ruler's reign. It was 1824 before all the words on the Rosetta Stone were correctly understood. The code was cracked by French genius Jean-François Champollion.

He started by matching known Greek letters on the third part with the Egyptian symbols on the first part. Then he counted and compared symbol frequency against other texts. The high number of ancient Egyptian hieroglyphs showed that they had to have several functions, representing sounds as well as objects and ideas.

▶ The Rosetta Stone has helped us to understand more about the amazing lives—and the even more amazing deaths—of the ancient Egyptians.

The top part was written in hieroglyphs, symbols that cover ancient Egyptian tombs and statues. No historian could work out what they meant.

The second part was written in Demotic, the everyday language of ancient Egypt. Another mystery.

The third part was written in ancient Greek, which people could understand. Finally, a key had been found to unlock the past.

Sir Henry to the rescue

In the 1830s and 40s, British scholar Sir Henry Rawlinson (1810–1895) became fascinated by carvings on Mount Behistun in Persia (modern Iran). The carvings were written in three ancient languages—Old Persian, Elamite, and Babylonian—and dated from the reign of King Darius the Great (548–486 BC). The inscriptions were written in cuneiform ("wedge-shaped") scripts. Rawlinson and others worked out that the Old Persian script represented sounds. They compared the symbols and their frequency to work out the other two scripts.

▶ Rawlinson risked his life climbing a sheer rockface to get a closer look at the carvings.

History mystery

Great civilizations thrived in the cities of the Indus Valley (modern Pakistan) more than 4,500 years ago. Thousands of objects have been decorated with symbols, but no one knows what they mean. There are few of the repeats and combinations that normally make up a language, but computer tests carried out in 2009 suggest that this really was an ancient script.

▶ There are said to be about 417 symbols in the Indus script.

IN 2011 A 21-VOLUME AKKADIAN DICTIONARY —MADE UP OF 28,000 CUNEIFORM WORDS—WAS PUBLISHED BY THE UNIVERSITY OF CHICAGO, U.S. IT TOOK 90 YEARS TO COMPLETE AND THE WORK INVOLVED 85 PEOPLE!

Back to the future

More than 3,000 years ago, Chinese fortune-tellers carved words onto animal bones and turtle shells, which they threw into a fire. As the bones cracked, the lines that appeared were believed to show glimpses of the future. These "oracle bone" scripts were ancestors of modern Chinese writing and provide historical information about the rulers of that period.

▶ When farmers dug up these bone fragments, thousands of years after they were carved, they thought they were magical dragon bones.

Some people believe that the Phaistos Disk is a forgery from 1908.

Secret spirals

The island of Crete, in southern Greece, has many ancient secrets, legends, and ruins. This clay disk was found at the ancient city of Phaistos and dates back to about 1700 BC. Its spirals of stamped designs have never been decoded. Some experts believe that a few of these symbols are similar to a mysterious Cretan script known as Linear A.

Out of the ASHES

Although ancient people associated volcanic eruptions with angry gods, they often settled nearby because volcanic soil is rich and fertile—it was worth the risk. Volcanoes are symbols of nature's destructive powers, but they sometimes preserve the remains of humans and buildings. These sites are precious time capsules, where a moment in the past is frozen for eternity.

Mega-blast!

One of the most cataclysmic eruptions in history tore apart the Greek island of Thira, or Santorini, near Crete, perhaps in the 1620s BC. The sea rushed in and flooded the vast hole that was left behind. On the surviving land, a town was buried beneath a volcanic stone called pumice. Excavations at this site, named Akrotiri, began in 1967. They revealed drains, furniture, pottery, and stunning paintings in the Minoan style of ancient Crete.

▶ Footprints from the distant past, uncovered by Paul Abell, a member of Mary Leakey's team, in 1978. These hominids not only walked upright, but had feet very like our own.

The footprints are 7–8.5 in (18.5–21.5 cm) long.

Fossilized footprints

These footprints at Laetoli in Tanzania look as if they were made only yesterday. In fact, they are about 3.7 million years old and were made long before modern humans had evolved. They belong to hominids, the family of creatures that includes our distant ancestors. The marks were made in fine volcanic ash, which then set hard after being moistened by rain. The footprints became fossilized, preserved forever in stone.

◀ The remains of Akrotiri reveal how the Minoan people lived more than 3,600 years ago.

▼ Plaster casts capture the moment at which people died in Pompeii.

Plastered!

The Italian city of Pompeii was buried under pumice and ash to a depth of up to 23 ft (7 m). Entire bodies became encased in the ash, leaving imprints as they decayed. Eventually only the skeletons remained. Archeologists discovered that by filling the cavities with plaster, they could recreate the citizens of Pompeii as they had appeared on that fateful day in AD 79.

POMPEII IN A FLASH

Imagine a whole city, stopped in its tracks in AD 79. Half-eaten meals are left on the table, dogs and people cower from the choking ash that showers down relentlessly. The city is entombed. Excavations at Pompeii have revealed the forum (marketplace), temples, streets, shops, houses, gardens, theaters, baths, taverns, laundries, and bakeries.

▼ This carbonized loaf of bread was found in an oven at Pompeii.

▼ This skeleton was excavated from the ruins of Herculaneum, with jeweled gold rings on its finger still intact.

HORRORS IN HERCULANEUM

Herculaneum was a small Italian seaside town just 4 mi (7 km) from Mount Vesuvius. The eruption of Vesuvius in AD 79 blasted it with ash and superhot water, burying the town under 50 ft (15 m) of boiling mud, which turned to rock. Many people fled before the disaster, but 300 or so were stranded in boathouses by the beach, trying to escape. Excavations since the 1700s have uncovered houses, public baths, fountains, jewelry, and wall paintings.

Can you imagine a modern city such as Sydney, Las Vegas, or Toronto being simply wiped off the map? How might such a site look to an archeologist in the future? Many thriving cities have been destroyed by floods, earthquakes, plague, or warfare. Sometimes climate change has turned fertile lands into deserts, which can no longer provide enough food to feed the city's inhabitants.

▶ Roots and tropical vines partially obscure the stonework of Angkor Wat.

Return of the wild

It takes no time at all for great monuments and cities to be reclaimed by nature. They become eroded by the wind, cracked by frost, or baked by the Sun. Roots and creepers take hold, covering, pushing, and concealing. In Cambodia, the awesome sites of Angkor Thom and the great temple of Angkor Wat, built in the 1100s to 1400s, would be swallowed up by tropical vegetation if they were not constantly cleared and maintained.

▶ Machu Picchu was built in about 1400 and abandoned after the Spanish invasion in 1532.

On the trail of the Incas

On steep mountain slopes in Peru there were mysterious traces of buildings and terraced fields, overgrown with trees and undergrowth. In 1911 an expedition led by the American archeologist Dr. Hiram Bingham (1875–1956) crossed the Urubamba River and climbed up toward the peak of Machu Picchu. Bingham began to clear the ruins and excavate. He discovered finely built stone houses, terraces, steep streets, temples, fountains, and workshops.

Sand and rock

Petra, in Jordan, was once the destination for camel caravans crossing the desert with their riches. The city was set in a cleft of rock and supplied with fresh water by aqueducts. Petra was the capital of the Nabataeans from the 500s BC and came under Roman rule in AD 106. Soon after, trade moved to coastal routes. The West didn't know of Petra's existence until 1812 when it was rediscovered by Johann Ludwig Burckhardt (1784–1817).

▲ Petra's buildings were carved directly from the sandstone rockface.

THE MOAT THAT SURROUNDS THE TEMPLE OF ANGKOR WAT IS 4 MI (6 KM) LONG.

Early life

Çatalhöyük in Turkey was one of the world's earliest towns, settled between about 7500 and 5700 BC. Its houses were joined together, with no streets in between. This was a center of farming, crafts, and religious rituals. It may have been abandoned when trading patterns changed.

◀ This statue of the Mother Goddess was made in Çatalhöyük in about 6000 BC.

ORDINARY OBJECTS

Discoveries of everyday items show historians how ordinary people lived their lives. We can relate these findings to our own lives to see how things have changed over the years.

1300s

Jar for scented oil
Makresia, Greece
Ancient Greeks kept cosmetics, ointments, scents, and oils in ornately decorated terra-cotta containers. Oils made their skin smooth and supple. Rich women also used face powder to achieve a fashionably pale complexion.

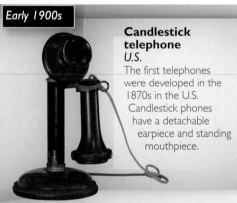

1700s

Maori comb
New Zealand
Maori men wore combs carved from whalebone or wood in their topknots (knot of hair arranged on the top of the head). The combs were regarded as sacred possessions.

Greek vase
Greece
Food and wine were stored in terra-cotta containers called amphorae. They kept goods cool.

Early 1900s

Candlestick telephone
U.S.
The first telephones were developed in the 1870s in the U.S. Candlestick phones have a detachable earpiece and standing mouthpiece.

EVERYDAY MEMORIES
The answers to questions about everyday life in the past are revealed by countless little clues. How did people dress and eat? Did they go to school? How did they make a living? How did they communicate with each other?

1900s

Phonograph
U.S.
Also called a gramophone, the phonograph could record and play music.

1400s

Aztec calendar stone
Mexico
This large stone shows details of months and historical ages.

Toy animals
Veracruz, Mexico
The Totonac people of Mexico made ceramic animal figures as toys for their children.

c. 1150

Roman glassware
Rheims, France
Useful glassware was manufactured in many parts of the Roman Empire. These jugs and vases come from ancient Gaul.

c. AD 150

c. AD 1850

Victorian clothes
U.K.
A bonnet, shawl, calico skirt, jacket, and ankle boots were typical working-class clothes in the Victorian era.

5th–6th century

RELIVING THE PAST
Historical reenactments are organized to educate people about the past by making them feel like they are there. Museums and castles often recreate historical scenes by staging displays with actors and actresses. Even schoolchildren can dress up as Romans for the day to get an insight into what life was like in ancient Rome.

1950s

Television
U.S.
The Philco Predicta was a classic set from the early days of television.

50 BC–AD 50

Bronze mirror
Desborough, England
This elegant mirror decorated in the Celtic artistic style dates from Britain's Iron Age.

DRESSING UP
Many schoolchildren get the chance to dress up when they go to visit a museum or a historical building. For just one day they can feel like Victorians, or like a Norman family in a medieval castle.

AD 395–632

Wool balls, knitting needle, spool, and spindle
Coptic, Egypt
Ancient Egyptians knitted woolen socks. They had two tubes at the end for their toes, so they could be worn with sandals.

Land of the DEAD

Funeral rituals were already taking place tens of thousands of years ago. The way in which dead bodies have been treated has varied greatly over the ages and among different cultures and religions. The dead person might be buried, cremated, exposed in the open, or preserved as a mummy.

The puzzle of the "Red Lady"

In 1823, a skeleton was found in a cave at Paviland in Wales, U.K., by William Buckland (1784–1856). It was surrounded by shell jewelry and covered in a kind of red ocher. It was immediately assumed that this was the burial of a Roman lady. However, we now know that it was actually a young male who lived just over 29,000 years ago, perhaps the chief of a band of hunters.

▲ The Paviland skeleton is the oldest known ceremonial burial in Western Europe.

◄ A gilded bronze oil lamp in the shape of a kneeling female servant, from the 2nd century BC, was found in the tomb of Princess Dou Wan.

▼ Dou Wan's suit was made up of 2,156 plates of jade.

The eternal princess

In China, princes and princesses were sometimes buried in beautiful suits made of small squares of jade bound by gold wire. This smooth, hard gemstone was believed to be magical, making the wearer immortal and preserving the body. Liu Sheng and his wife, Dou Wan, were buried in about 113 BC. Her tomb contained more than 3,000 precious items.

The grave robbers of Thebes

The trouble with filling the tombs of the dead with fabulous riches is that they attract thieves. To avoid this, the Egyptians began to bury their dead pharaohs in a secret necropolis (burial ground) in the cliffs near the city of Thebes (modern Luxor). Although the "Valley of the Kings," as it became known, was guarded day and night, robbers still managed to break into the tombs and steal the gold.

▲ Grave robbers risked their lives to steal the treasure of the pharaohs.

◀ This statue of a ram from Ur is made of gold, silver, shell, and a blue stone called lapis lazuli.

The royal tombs of Ur

Ur was a city in Mesopotamia (ancient Iraq). Digs in the 1920s revealed 16 royal tombs dating from 2600 to 2500 BC. They were packed with treasure, including golden crowns, gaming boards, a lyre, and exquisite jewelry.

A funeral for a Viking

The Vikings were a seafaring people, so it is not surprising that they often chose to end their days at sea. The bodies of Viking chieftains might be burned in their boats, or gravestones might be laid out in the shape of a boat. This superb longship was found buried under an earthen mound at Oseberg in Norway. It contained the bodies of two women who died in AD 834. One of them may have been a queen.

▼ The Oseberg ship contained dresses, veils, and other textiles, as well as finely carved chests, wooden sleighs, a cart, and the remains of horses, dogs, and an ox.

THE TOMBS OF UR ALSO INCLUDED DEATH PITS, WHERE MANY SERVANTS HAD BEEN SACRIFICED TO ACCOMPANY THE DEAD KINGS AND QUEENS TO THE NEXT WORLD.

Faces of

FOREVER

Some bodies are preserved naturally after death because of the conditions where they are buried. Others have been preserved on purpose for religious reasons, as some cultures believed it would allow the deceased to travel to the afterlife in one piece. The Egyptians perfected this skill.

▼ This mummy from Saqqara was discovered after 2,600 years.

In the land of deserts

Burials in desert sands can dry out dead bodies naturally. This is perhaps how the Egyptians first learned about mummification. They soon developed an elaborate process for preserving corpses artificially, using natron salt, cedar oil, resin, and bandages.

IN THE MIDDLE AGES, MUMMIES FROM RAIDED TOMBS WERE GROUND UP AND USED FOR MAKING MAGICAL POTIONS AND OINTMENTS.

Farewell, Artemidorus

When Egypt came under Greek and then Roman rule, dead bodies were still being mummified and buried in beautiful wooden coffins, which were shaped like human bodies. They were fitted with panels bearing very realistic portraits to provide a reminder of the deceased.

◄ This mummy case from Hawara shows the face of a young man called Artemidorus, who died about 1,900 years ago.

Towers of the dead

Mummification was common in the deserts and mountains of Chile and Peru from 5000 BC until the AD 1400s. In the plateaus of the high Andes, mummies were left in stone towers called chullpas, along with food, drink, knives, pots, and mirrors. In South America, mummies of children were sometimes placed in pottery urns and buried beneath the floor of the family home. Loving parents wanted them to be close at hand, where they could care for their spirit.

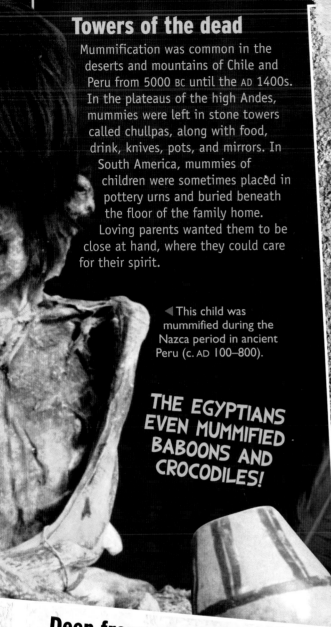

◄ This child was mummified during the Nazca period in ancient Peru (c. AD 100–800).

THE EGYPTIANS EVEN MUMMIFIED BABOONS AND CROCODILES!

THE BODIES IN THE BOG

The best-surviving bodies of all have been found in peaty wetlands. In the bogs of northern Europe, the cold, acidic conditions and a lack of oxygen have preserved the skin and organs. The bodies date from about 8000 BC to the early medieval period, but most are from the 5th to 1st century BC. Historians believe that they may have been violently killed as sacrifices to the gods.

► A bog man from Lindow Moss, in England. He may have been sacrificed about 2,000 years ago.

Deep frozen

Ice has preserved corpses in the perpetually cold soil of Siberia, and in the mountain glaciers of Europe's Alps—just as if they have been kept in a natural freezer. In 1991 the body of a hunter from Europe's Copper Age was found on the border of Italy and Austria. It had been preserved in a glacier and was given the nickname of Ötzi the Iceman.

◄ The Iceman is the oldest complete human mummy ever to be found. He is so well preserved, even his eyes are still visible.

VISAS   11

Name: Ötzi

Date of birth: c. 3300 BC

Place of Residence: The Alps, Europe

Age at time of death: c. 45 years

Height: 5ft 5 in (1.65 m)

Weight: 110 lb (50 kg)

Distinguishing marks: Tattoos (or needle treatment)

Dress: Bearskin cap, cloak, leather coat, belt, leggings, and shoes

Possessions: Flint knife, bow and arrows, copper ax

HISTORY Lab

S cience and technology have transformed the work of historians and archeologists. Special techniques can be used to determine what people ate just before they died, the cause of death, and even what type of work they did. They even reveal what the climate and plant life were like thousands of years ago.

◄ As a tree grows it produces more layers of cells, or rings, in its trunk. These can provide clues about past climates.

It's all in the trunk

Dendrochronology is the scientific term for counting the annual growth rings in wood. The number of rings offers an accurate year count. The width of the rings provides information about climate and growing conditions.

Genetic tools

DNA is the chemical code of inheritance in all living things and genetics is now a vital tool in archeology. As well as helping to identify a mummy, DNA analysis can also give historians a greater understanding of the time in which the person lived. Diseases the mummy suffered from and medicines it took, as well as its family lineage can also be discovered.

► DNA tests suggest that this is the mummy of Hatshepsut, an Egyptian queen who ruled as pharaoh in the 15th century BC.

◄ A sample for carbon dating is taken from a reindeer bone.

Radioactive material

Elements that break down naturally give out radiation. They are said be "radioactive." Organic remains such as wood, grain, textiles, or bones contain both radioactive carbon-14 atoms and stable carbon-12 atoms, which can be compared. The older the object, the less radioactive it will be.

A microscopic triumph

An electron microscope was used to study three tiny grains of pollen found in the stomach of the mummy Ötzi the Iceman. This gave archeologists information about where and when Ötzi died, including the local climate and vegetation, and the season. Electron microscopes were also used to identify food particles in his gut.

▶ Ötzi's last breakfast had been a type of wheat, probably made into a coarse bread.

Call in the dentist

Teeth are the hardest, toughest part of the human body. They often survive long after the bones have rotted away. By studying just one tooth and its wear and tear, it is possible to build up a picture of a person's life. Age, diet, methods of food preparation, general health, stress levels, hygiene, evidence of famine, and lines of descent can all be revealed.

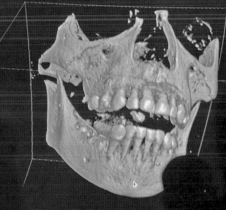

▲ A CT (computer tomography) scan is used to create digital models of a child's jaw and teeth from its 2,000-year-old mummy.

▼ This naturally mummified body dates from the 1700s and was taken from a church crypt in Hungary. Scans showed that the cause of death was tuberculosis.

Scans and X-rays

In hospitals, patients can be examined using X-rays and a variety of other scanning technology. This equipment is perfect for examining fragile mummies or other remains. Even removing the delicate bandaging of a mummy can be disastrous, but an X-ray can see straight through to the bone or the skull without causing damage.

SELECT PATIENT FOR 3D DISPLAY
VERIFY PATIENT INFORMATION
SELECT CONTOUR FILE
SELECT PROCESS MODE
ON LINE 3D
SELECT 3D IMAGE TYPE
SELECT IMAGE RESOLUTION
SELECT SLICE SEPARATION
SELECT LIGHT SOURCE ANGLE
VOLUME
DISPLAY 3D VIEW
SAVE
RESTORE
ANNOTATE
TOGGLE BGND BLUE/BLACK
SELECT ROTATION ANGLE USING METER ON LEFT

TURN ANGLE = -50

▲ These scans were taken through the closed coffin of an Egyptian temple singer who lived in about 950 BC.

Treasure Trove

Finds of treasure involve fabulous wealth, precious objects, dazzling beauty, and tales of greed and robbery. Valuable discoveries can inform historians about past societies. They learn how things were made and what was considered to be valuable.

HIDDEN HOARDS

Treasure was often hidden in secret places. People may have been smuggling stolen loot, hiding their riches from an invading army, or safely "banking" their money. If the owners were killed or forced to flee before they could reclaim their hoard, its whereabouts may be lost for centuries.

▲ A Viking treasure hoard from about AD 860, found at Hon, in Norway.

▲ The Crusaders shipped the bronze horses back to Venice, Italy, where they became one of the city's most famous sights.

THE SACKING OF A CITY

In 1204, a Christian army of Venetian and French Crusaders bound for the Middle East turned aside to launch a brutal attack on the Christian city of Constantinople (modern Istanbul). They sacked the great churches and palaces, stealing silver, gold, precious stones, pearls, silk textiles, and sacred relics. They carried off a vast fortune and even stole the magnificent statues of horses from the city's racetrack.

FROM THE TOMBS OF LORDS

Many of the most dazzling treasures from all over the world have been found in the tombs and graves of royalty or high-ranking nobles. Grave goods may have been intended as objects for the dead to take to the afterlife, or they may be items of religious ritual or badges of rank.

◀ The Moche "Lord" of Sipán, who lived in Peru about 1,800 years ago, was buried in a pyramid along with gold, silver, and 400 jewels.

CROWN JEWELS

Kings, queens, and emperors liked to display their status and wealth with ceremonial treasures, called regalia, that they wore or carried. Often made of gold or covered in jewels, they included crowns, tiaras, diadems, chains, swords, rings, gloves, orbs (globes), scepters (ornamental staffs), and ermine-trimmed cloaks. Historical crown jewels—or duplicates—are often put on display.

GIFTS FOR THE GODS

People have always made offerings to their spirits or gods, such as incense, sacrifices, or food. "Votive" offerings may also have included fine weapons or jewelry, thrown into a sacred pool or left at a shrine. Medieval rulers would try to win divine favor by giving rich treasures to temples, monasteries, or churches.

◀ The Guarrazar treasure contained crowns, sapphires, and pearls. It was given to the Church in the 600s AD, by Germanic kings who ruled in Spain.

▲ This crown, orb, and scepter were owned by the kings of Poland.

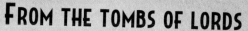
ABOUT 3,000 OF THE OLDEST GOLD ITEMS WERE FOUND IN VARNA, BULGARIA, DATING FROM 4700-4200 BC.

Return to the BATTLEFIELD

Wartime memorabilia, eyewitness accounts, and historical records help archeologists to build a picture of the realities of wartime. Sometimes their research can reveal forgotten stories, correct inaccurate records, or add significant material to historical archives.

MAPPING THE CONFLICT

Army maps of the time help archeologists and historians locate battlefield sites, tunnels, and trenches. Archeologists are then able to produce modern maps based on their discoveries.

	French line
	Canadian line
	British line
	Central Division (British)
●●●	Cavalry Corps which took the place of the Central Division on May 13
	"A" Division (British; originally Colonel Geddes' mixed brigade)

◄ In World War I, the Belgian city of Ypres was destroyed during repeated battles.

Fading photographs

Traveling back to World War I (1914–1918) is made easier by the widespread use of photography at that time. We can see the expressions on the faces of the young men on both sides as they marched to the front line, lived in the mud of the trenches, and went into battle—history as it actually happened.

► Albert "Smiler" Marshall (on horseback) survived World War I and lived until 2005.

Letters and diaries

The authentic voices of World War I soldiers have survived in their diaries and in the letters sent home from the front line, even those that were censored for security reasons by the military authorities.

30

Digging into history

Both sides fighting in World War I (the Allies and the Central Powers) dug networks of trenches to protect their troops, from the North Sea to Switzerland. Archeologists in the Somme region of France dig the battlefield sites to discover the exact position of the trenches of 1916. Archeological finds include skeletons, uniform buttons and badges, helmets, and the remains of weapons, bullets, and shells.

English Miles

Shaded area indicates ground won by Germans as a result of the first great gas attack.

► British author Michael Morpurgo visits the Flanders Field Museum in Ypres.

▲ Remains of soldiers who fell during the horrific battles of 1916 are still being uncovered today.

MUSEUMS TELL THE STORY

War was a confusing and terrifying experience for many of the troops on the ground. They could not know the bigger picture of World War I as it progressed. Today, historians can research the tactics and strategies of the generals and the everyday life of the troops by visiting museums and battlefields.

Remembering the soldiers

Cemeteries and memorials are found all over the battlefields of World War I. The huge scale of these burial grounds is a sobering sight. The graves are still visited by descendants of the soldiers who died, and they also provide useful information for war historians.

▲ The names of over 54,000 missing soldiers are recorded on the Menin Gate Memorial in Ypres.

OCEAN Depths

Another world exists beneath the waves. Amid sandbanks and coral reefs, marine archeologists search for the remains of ancient shipwrecks—the victims of storms or naval battles long ago. These are precious time capsules, but are often difficult to access in deep, dangerous waters.

Titanic!

"Titanic" means gigantic, and this was the name given to a state-of-the-art, trans-Atlantic, luxury liner a century ago. In 1912, on its maiden voyage, the ship struck an iceberg and went down with the loss of more than 1,500 lives. It became the most famous shipwreck of all time. In 1985, the remains of *Titanic* were discovered at a depth of nearly 2.5 mi (4 km). More than 6,000 items, including plates and the ship's whistle, have been recovered.

▲ A submersible's camera reveals the rails of the *Titanic*.

Classical cargo

The ancient Greeks were great seafarers and colonists, trading all over the Mediterranean Sea and the Black Sea from the 9th century BC. Wrecks reveal shipbuilding and navigation methods, while surviving cargoes tell us about trading patterns, economics, and even Greek art. Finds include amphorae, the large pottery jars used to store wine and oil.

◀ This is the world's earliest known mechanical computer, dating back to about 100 BC. It was discovered in a Greek shipwreck.

The *Mary Rose* is raised from the seabed in a giant mechanical cradle.

The lost warship

Back in 1545, the warship *Mary Rose* was the pride of the English navy and of King Henry VIII. She was fitted with new "gun ports," openings in the ship's side that allowed the firing of heavy cannon. Sailing out to meet the French fleet, *Mary Rose* flooded and sank. The wreck was found in 1971, many of its timbers preserved under the seabed.

Treasure galleons

After Spanish soldiers invaded Central and South America in the 1500s, they shipped a fortune in looted treasure back to Spain. Between 1566 and 1789, they organized convoys of big sailing ships called galleons to set out from the Caribbean Sea across the Atlantic Ocean. Many ships in these treasure fleets were attacked by pirates, or sunk by hurricanes. The *Nuestra Señora de Atocha* was part of a fleet wrecked on coral reefs off Florida, U.S., in 1622. This ship, with its precious cargo, coins, and cannon, was found in 1985 by American treasure hunters.

▶ This ring and Spanish coin were salvaged from the wreck of a pirate ship, the *Whydah*, which sank off Cape Cod, in North America, in 1717.

IN 1967, DIVERS LOCATED A GREEK CITY THAT SANK BENEATH THE WAVES ABOUT 3,000 YEARS AGO. REMAINS FROM THE PAVLOPETRI SITE HAVE BEEN DATED TO BETWEEN 2800 AND 1200 BC.

Air to GROUND

Archeologists have found the most awesome historical sites—from the air! Images of Earth from air or space can reveal ancient patterns of fields, settlements, or earthworks that could never be seen from the ground. These show the whole of a historic site in its landscape, revealing its overall layout and features.

▼ A microlight aircraft flies over the landscape of Wiltshire in England, which is world famous for its prehistoric monuments.

In the early Middle Ages, Avebury village was built across part of the henge.

High above Avebury

From the ground, the site of Avebury, Wiltshire, U.K., is impressive. From the air, it makes sense. Earthworks form a great ring containing three circles of standing stones. This "henge" was raised from about 2850 BC to 2200 BC, during the New Stone Age. Archeologists believe that it was originally used for ceremonies or rituals.

Stonehenge revealed

The plan of Stonehenge becomes very clear from the air. The position of the great stones and the outer earthworks is emphasized by light and shadow. The site is part of a much larger sacred and ceremonial landscape.

▲ A view never seen during the first 4,900 years of Stonehenge's existence.

Monkey puzzle

Scratched out of the soil in Peru's Nazca Desert are huge patterns and pictures of birds, animals, and people. It was not until the invention of aircraft that people could really see these for what they were. They date back to AD 400–650 and may represent messages to the gods or ceremonial pathways.

▲ This Nazca Desert drawing shows a gigantic monkey with a curly tail.

SOME OF THE NAZCA DRAWINGS ARE AN ENORMOUS 660 FT (200 M) ACROSS!

▶ Found in Ohio, U.S., the first recorded sightings of the Great Serpent Mound are from the 1800s.

Snaking through the landscape

The Great Serpent Mound is the largest animal-shaped mound, or effigy, in the world, at 1,348 ft (411 m) long and up to 3 ft (one meter) high. It is believed to have been built by the Native Americans in AD 1070. After excavating the site, researchers now believe that it was not a burial site.

Rebuilding HISTORY

History can easily be destroyed or lost. Wood rots, stone and brick crumble, costumes deteriorate, written records are easily torn, and precious metals may be stolen and melted down. Saving and recovering the evidence of history is crucial—using conservation, restoration, and reconstruction.

BEFORE

AFTER

▶ Shards of pottery may be carefully reassembled and stuck together.

Jigsaw puzzles

Imagine a vase shattered into a thousand fragments, or an ancient scroll that has disintegrated into a handful of scraps. Often all that remains of a helmet, shield, or bowl are a few crumbling strips of bronze. Experts spend many hours putting together the pieces of the jigsaw, from which pieces may be missing. Sometimes it is not known what the object is until the puzzle is completed.

▼ A painting by Guido Reni (1575–1642) is carefully restored.

BEFORE

AFTER

Canvas and paint

Restoring precious paintings requires painstaking care. Removing centuries of grime or varnish may reveal the colors in startling freshness, or even cast doubt on who painted the picture in the first place. X-rays may reveal corrections the artist has made while painting, or changes that others have made later. Pigments or canvas repairs must be carefully matched with the originals.

BEFORE

BOMB DESTRUCTION

In 1945, as World War II (1939–1945) was drawing to a close, the historical city of Dresden in Germany was razed to the ground by Allied bombing and by a raging firestorm that followed. Decades of reconstruction and restoration began in 1951. The city's great domed church, the Frauenkirche, was completely rebuilt to the exact specifications of the original.

▼ The Frauenkirche lay in ruins after 1945.

AFTER

▼ Reconstruction was completed in 2004–2005.

BEFORE

▼ The temple and statues are cut into blocks of stone, some weighing up to 30 tons each.

AFTER

▶ The temples are now safe in their new position. This feat was carried out by engineers and archeologists for UNESCO (The United Nations Educational, Scientific, and Cultural Organization).

The Abu Simbel story

Completed in 1224 BC, a great temple complex towered over the Nile valley in southern Egypt. Its twin temples were dedicated to the pharaoh Ramesses II and his wife Nefertari. In the 1950s, a new dam was to be built at Aswan. Unless urgent action was taken, the Abu Simbel site would be flooded by the rising waters of the Nile. From 1963–1968 the entire complex was taken apart, raised to a new, safe position, and rebuilt.

TEMPLES OF TIME

We can't all visit lost cities or discover treasure, but we can go to local historical sites, museums, and galleries. They act as centers of education, research, conservation, and debate. Curators and archivists recreate scenes from the past using real objects and showcase awesome artifacts used by people, hundreds or thousands of years ago.

▶ See the record-breaking American plane *Spirit of St. Louis* (1927) at Washington's National Air and Space Museum.

Get inspired
Designers can get their inspiration from the many fashions of the past. Many museums around the world have stunning displays of historic dress, stage costumes, and fine jewelry.

▲ Fine tapestries from France's National Museum of the Middle Ages, in Paris.

Treasures from around the world
Some of the most famous museums are the Louvre in Paris, France, the Metropolitan Museum of Art in New York City, U.S., the British Museum in London, U.K., and the Smithsonian Museums (19 are located in Washington D.C., U.S.). Exhibits full of historical treasures may be seen from all over the world. Although exciting for visitors, this can be a matter of international dispute as some people believe that treasures should be returned to their homeland.

▲ A ballgown worn by Queen Victoria in 1851 was shown at the Queen's Gallery of Buckingham Palace in London, U.K.

All at sea

Barcelona's medieval royal shipyard is the historic setting for a splendid maritime museum packed with historical ships from ornate galleys to fishing boats. Like many museums it tells you much more besides—about mapping and navigation, political history, trade, and economics.

▼ A replica of the 1568 Royal Galley of Don John of Austria.

Totem poles

Museums of anthropology introduce us to human societies and cultures of the past. This totem pole, made by the Haida people, is from the collection at the University of British Columbia, in Canada. In the 1800s, tall wooden carvings were symbols of power, prestige, and family groups.

◀ Ethnic carvings from long ago still inspire many modern artists and sculptors.

▲ Ancient Babylon's Processional Way (c. 575 BC) is recreated at the Pergamon Museum in Berlin, Germany.

INDEX